Kat

Endogo book 2

Published by Crossbridge Books
Worcester
© Crossbridge Books 2025

ISBN 978-1-916945-11-1

British Library Cataloguing Publication Data. A catalogue record for this book is available from the British Library.

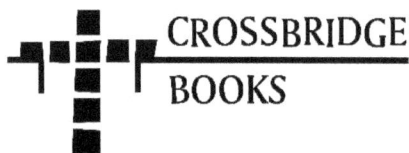

CROSSBRIDGE
BOOKS

Kat

Endogo book 2

by R M Price-Mohr

Vocabulary for book 2:

and
are
at/Kat
bird
eat
fish
found
fruit
goes
going
green
has
into
like
of
some
they/They
this/This
to
with

Foreword for teachers

These books have been developed for older beginner readers. The research-based approach focuses on the recognition of just 100 key words that together make up approximately two-thirds of all reading matter in English.

For each new book, twenty new words are introduced and listed at the beginning of each book The new vocabulary for each book should be introduced to the learner in such a way that they will be able to recognise them at sight <u>before</u> reading the book. It is recommended that this is achieved through playing with the printed words. In the first instance, this should be by having two sets of printed and separated words in large font (minimum 20 point) that the beginner reader can match. It is crucial that the teacher continuously verbalise the words, and they may point to significant features in words, firstly the initial letters and secondly to any other distinctive features, to assist with the matching. Following this, the word recognition can be reinforced in games such as bingo, dominoes, snap, Pelmanism etc.

It is crucial that the teacher continue to verbalise the words during all the games, and the teacher should draw attention to the first letter of words and sound out that initial letter for the beginner.

Some temptations to avoid:

- Do not ask the reader to sound out all the individual letters of a word — only the initial letter has value at this stage for reading.
- Do not test the reader to see if they can recognise any of the words by telling you what they say — this should become obvious during the games; remember that visual recognition is not the same thing as verbalising what is seen.

The island.

The green rain forest.

Max goes into a cave.

This is Kat.

Kat has found a small fish to eat.

Kat the endogo is at home.

The home is in the cave.

Max has found some fruit to eat with the fish.

They are going to eat the food.

The bird has some of the fruit.

Kat and Max like the food.

They are happy.

High Frequency Words:

are
at
bird
goes
going
green
into
of
some
they
this
to
with

Word patterns:

_at	at
	Kat
_ing	looking
	Eating
	going

www.ingramcontent.com/pod-product-compliance
Lightning Source LLC
LaVergne TN
LVHW010316070426

835510LV00024B/3406